CW00920707

ANIMAL TALK

WRITTEN BY

Dr. Michael Leach and Dr. Meriel Lland

ILLUSTRATED BY

Asia Orlando

DK | Penguin Random House

Authors Dr. Michael Leach, Dr. Meriel Lland
Illustrator Asia Orlando
Editor Kieran Jones
Acquisitions Editor James Mitchem
Designers Sonny Flynn, Charlotte Jennings,
Charlotte Milner, Bettina Myklebust Stovne
Design assistance Sif Nørskov
Production Editor Dragana Puvacic
Production Controller Magda Bojko
Jacket and Sales Material Coordinator Magda Pszuk
Jacket Designer Charlotte Milner
Managing Art Editor Di Peyton Jones
Publishing Director Sarah Larter

First published in Great Britain in 2023 by
Dorling Kindersley Limited
DK, One Embassy Gardens, 8 Viaduct Gardens,
London, SW11 7BW

The authorised representative in the EEA is
Dorling Kindersley Verlag GmbH. Arnulfstr. 124,
80636 Munich, Germany

Illustrations © Asia Orlando 2022
Copyright in the layouts and design of
the Work shall be vested in the Publisher.
Dorling Kindersley Limited
DK, a Division of Penguin Random House LLC
10 9 8 7 6 5 4 3 2 1
001–335668–July/2023

A CIP catalogue record for this book
is available from the British Library.
ISBN: 978-0-2416-2031-1

Printed and bound in China

For the curious
www.dk.com

MIX
Paper | Supporting
responsible forestry
FSC™ C018179

This book was made with Forest
Stewardship Council ™ certified
paper – one small step in DK's
commitment to a sustainable future.

For more information go to
www.dk.com/our-green-pledge

CONTENTS

WHAT IS COMMUNICATION?

When it comes to communication, whether animal or human, 'talk' is only part of the story. There are nearly 7,000 languages spoken today, yet just around 7 per cent of human communication is verbal.

Alongside the spoken word, body language (information shared through gestures such as a wave of the hand and a smile) plus scents and behaviours account for the other 93 per cent.

Non-human animals, like birds, bugs, and marvellous mammals, have even more ways to communicate with their families, friends, competitors, and enemies. Animal 'talk' is about so much more than words.

The science of animal communication – the giving and sharing of important information – is full of the unexpected. Did you know that elephants hear through their feet? Or that a penguin can identify a chick's voice from 100,000 other baby chick squeaks? There are golden beetles that turn red when scared, and crocodiles that use birdy toothpicks to keep their breath fresh! Let's explore some of the most surprising, exciting, sneaky, and strange examples of how animals communicate – with each other, and with us.

WHY DO ANIMALS COMMUNICATE?

Communication helps animals survive and live their best lives! Animal comms help them to find food, find mates, establish who's boss, guard their territory, coordinate the team, and care for their young. They use a whole box of tricks to achieve their goals – sound, visuals, touch, taste, and smell.

TEAMWORK

Pods of orca whales are precision predators and have complex hunting strategies. Using calls, whistles, nudges, and demonstrations, elders teach calves the tactics of the hunt. Everyone has a role in the team.

SHOWING WHO'S BOSS

Silverback gorillas make sure everyone knows who's in charge of the troop by roaring and beating their chest noisily.

CHILDCARE

'Ready or not, here I come!' say the baby crocodiles from inside their eggs. Their version is more a chirpy 'umph' call but it tells mum and the other babies it's time. Mum then digs them out from their sandy nest in a mass hatching. She'll even carry them to the water's edge in her mouth!

GUARDING TERRITORY

Guanacos leave HUGE piles of poop at the edges of their territory to show exactly who owns what!

FINDING FOOD

Think 'sharing' is just for humans? Think again. When times are hard, azure-winged magpies beg for snacks from their friends. Their hungry 'kwink-kwink-kwink' calls and chick-like wing flutters work like magic!

IMPRESSING A MATE

Peacocks know exactly how to flirt! Their raucous screams and super-stunning tails impress and attract peahens. As the tail opens, it quivers, rustles, and vibrates the air, holding the peahens' attention.

PEAHEN

PEACOCK

ROOSTER

COCK-A-DOODLE-DO-ING

Roosters are male chickens. They have BIG alarm-clock voices to wake up the flock with a 'come and get it' breakfast call or 'crow'. The 'cock-a-doodle-do' call tells everyone this territory is taken! Roosters also often crow just before nightfall to gather the flock into the safety of the coop or trees. It takes a rooster up to eight months to learn to crow.

GOOD VIBRATIONS

Sound is a communication favourite in the natural world, and chickens are no exception. Clucking, cackling, growling, squawking – chickens are great talkers! Their 30 vocalizations mean things like 'morning', 'help', or 'I'm fine'. As chickens have a strict social order, with the rooster and lead hen at the top, this language helps them maintain their bonds with other chickens.

CHICKENS

CLEVER CONVERSATIONS

When a rooster finds food, he makes a 'tuk, tuk, tuk' sound that attracts the hens to the feast. A similar sound is made by mother hens when they find treats for their chicks. Adults have language so complex they can indicate a predator attacking from the sky or on land. Like human babies, chicks have to learn to speak like grown-ups.

We measure sound in decibels. A rooster's crow is as loud as a dog's bark – around 90 decibels.

YELLOWHAMMER

TOMAYTO, TOMATO

Some birds 'talk' with accents! Songbirds learn to sing like their parents, and so experts can identify where a migrant bird comes from by its voice. Male yellowhammers were brought to New Zealand from England in the 1860s and it still speaks with a 'British' accent today.

WHITE BELLBIRD

TOP OF THE VOICE CHARTS

The white bellbird lives in the Amazon rainforest and has the loudest bird voice in the world – 125 decibels! Pretty much as loud as a rock concert!

SOUND IDEAS

Many animals use noise to send other animals – some friendly, some not – a message. Whether it's raising the alarm or just a friendly greeting, getting these messages across is vitally important.

A lion's roar can be as loud as 114 decibels and can be heard from 8 km (5 miles) away.

TESTING, TESTING, 123

When a lion wants to test the strength and togetherness of a rival pride, it walks up to them confidently and gets close (but not too close) and roars loudly and ferociously at them. This show of strength tells the onlooking group of lions that this challenger means business and may engage with them directly if the pride shows any sign of weakness.

HOWLER MONKEY

Howler monkeys have some of the LOUDEST calls in the whole animal kingdom. They live in small troops and come together at sunrise to make a deafening riot of calls. This warns other monkeys to steer clear of the troop's range. Howlers call with mouths wide open and make a whooping sound. Surprisingly, they don't like rain and will howl mournfully during storms.

INTIMIDATION FACTOR

In order to face down a threat from a plucky solo challenger, the pride of lions work together to put on a convincing performance. They roar back aggressively together in the hope that their greater numbers, and the sheer volume of their combined roar, will make their competitor think twice about taking them on.

LIVING IT LOUD

Think BIG sounds are all about BIG voices? Think again. Some of the loudest sounds in the animal world are made by the smallest creatures like grasshoppers, and they do it without even opening their mouths!

SCRATCHY RHYTHMS

The grasshopper's summery chirping sounds are made by rubbing together their back legs and wings.

AFRICAN CICADA

The world's loudest insect is the African cicada. Its call is as loud as a motorbike engine at close range.

FEEL THE SCRAPE

On their long hind legs, hoppers have a row of bumps that are scraped backwards and forwards across the wing. This is called 'stridulation'. It sounds a bit like the noise your thumbnail makes scratching over the teeth of a comb. Grasshoppers don't have ears like humans; instead, they sense the stridulation vibrations in their abdomen.

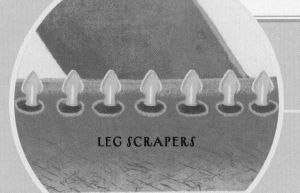

LEG SCRAPERS

GRASSHOPPER CHORUS

Hopper soloists make great sound, but if you want to pump up the volume, a choir might be the way to go! Cone-headed grasshoppers do just that. They sound off together to create a stridulation chorus that can be heard from far away. The louder the chorus, the more potential mates are attracted to the hoppers. Their loud and proud stridulations basically say: "here we are" and "come find us"!

DEMON MOLE RAT

Grumpy demon mole rats live in East Africa and spend their lives patrolling underground tunnels searching for plant roots to eat. They are not the most sociable of creatures – they don't like company and tend to fight when they meet. Mole rats avoid confrontations by thumping their heads hard on the burrow roof as a warning to others: "Stay away, this burrow's taken". We call this 'seismic communication'.

HIGH IN THE TREES

Tarsiers are tiny, goggle-eyed, leaping primates. Shy and nocturnal, they live in the forests of Asia. When tarsiers feel safe and secure, they chatter in high-pitched squeaks. But when the tarsiers feel threatened, they shift their calls up to a pitch that is too high for most animals to hear. This allows them to find each other in the dark without revealing their locations to potential predators.

UP UP UP

Some animals communicate using super high-frequency sounds. Those calls that are beyond the upper range of most human hearing we call 'ultrasounds'. Children, dogs, bats, dolphins, and mice hear ultrasound much better than adult humans.

TARSIER

TARSIER DETECTORS

Throughout the night, male and female tarsiers duet, calling together to strengthen their bonds. When the pair sing, they open their mouths wide but people hear nothing. Scientists use a kind of bat-detector to pick up their sounds and convert them to a pitch that we can hear. We can now listen to them chatter, call, and shout to each other.

HOLE-IN-THE-HEAD FROG

Tadpoles of the hole-in-the-head frog have special suckers on their bodies to help them stick to slippery rocks.

JUMPING WATERFALLS

Hole-in-the-head frogs live in the forests of Borneo, close to fast-flowing rivers or waterfalls. Other frogs communicate with croaks, whistles, and grunts, but the non-stop sound of rushing water makes too much noise for these calls to be heard. Hole-in-the-head frogs are the only ones that call in ultrasound. They make high-pitched squeaks that others can hear clearly above the roar of rushing water.

OCEAN CHORUS

Sound travels at 1,225 kph (761 mph) in air, but it goes much further and four times faster in water. This explains why whales can hear each other on opposite sides of the world!

WHALE SONG

Male humpback whales are one of the world's chattiest animals. They whisper, shriek, moan, grunt, and even produce a sound like a gunshot. This is whale song. We can listen to whale song with special equipment called hydrophones. Sometimes they pick up dozens of singing whales. One humpback was recorded for seven hours non-stop!

HUMPBACK WHALE

FIN-TASTIC CHOIR

Whale songs have many different meanings. The humpback's 'whup' sound is the way that whales say "hi". They give out special calls before feeding, often to tell others what food is available, just like people might do in a lunch queue. Alaskan humpbacks have a call that is used just for herring. Each whale group – or pod – has its own team song.

Breaching shows a humpback's fitness to potential mates.

CALF

Humpback mothers and babies whisper together in squeaks to avoid being heard by predators.

BOTTLENOSE DOLPHIN

Bottlenose dolphins generally make clicks and whistles. Clicks are used for echolocation, sounds that bounce off objects and let dolphins understand their surroundings. Whistles mean they want company, are frightened, or feel hungry.

HELLO THERE

Humpbacks breach to send messages far away. They jump clear of the water and twist in the air before crashing back into the sea, creating a giant splash. Angry humpbacks slap their tails on the surface of the water, this technique is called 'lobbing'.

To deter a rival, humpbacks 'lob' their tails violently.

17

EAR TALK

Wolf ears do more than just listen. Wolves let their ears do the talking! If their ears are up and their teeth are bared, it means they are angry. If their ears are back and their eyes are squinted, it means suspicion, and if their ears are flattened against the head, they are afraid.

SHOWING SUSPICION

SHOWING ANGER

TALKING TOGETHER

Animals that live alone have a limited need for communication. But sociable species are much more 'talkative'. Wolves inhabit a complex social world – they play, argue, share food, and protect each other within the pack. Just like people, to keep their society strong they communicate all the time. They use sounds, scents, and posture to stay connected.

A TALE OF TAILS

At close range, wolves communicate using body language. By moving their ears or holding their body in different positions, wolves reveal their mood, aggression level, or status in the group. The top dog – or alpha male – carries his tail high. A wolf threatening an attack holds its tail almost level with its spine, while lower-ranking wolves carry their tails down, sometimes between their hind legs.

LOWER-RANKING WOLF

ALPHA MALE

HOWLING WOLF

CALL OF THE WILD

Wolves howl to send signals long distance. A lost wolf listens to the pack's howls to find a way home. Howling together can be a team-building exercise; a way of shouting, "Go us!" Or a way to claim a territory: "This is our forest". They also use stinky scents in urine and poop to mark their territory. Every wolf's voice is unique. Scientists can identify a single individual from the howl as accurately as we can humans by their fingerprints.

If wolf chat seems familiar, remember pet dogs inherited most of their language from their wolf ancestors!

PLAY BOW

MOTHER AND PUPS

VOCAL ACTION

Wolves bark, whimper, growl, and howl to show their mood. Barking might mean danger! Warnings are often growled. A mother wolf calling cubs to suckle might whimper.

When family members meet, they nuzzle noses and rub their front teeth together in a kind of kiss.

DOG TOWN

Prairie dogs are full of surprises. They're not dogs at all, but a type of rodent related to squirrels. They live in North America in cool colonies called 'dog towns' and the ways they communicate are simply amazing.

LET'S PARTY

Constantly communicating, prairie dogs are real party animals! They live in a vast network of tunnels beneath grassland where they share food, groom each other, and scamper around foraging. To shout hello to distant neighbours they produce a long 'weeee-ooooo' greeting.

FERRUGINOUS HAWK

PRAIRIE DOG

The prairie dog's name comes from its warning bark that sounds like a small dog yapping.

EARLY-WARNING SYSTEM

Prairie dogs are all about family and keeping each other safe. They do this using a very specific vocal language. Their warning chirps don't just announce that a predator is near, they name the enemy, its colour, whether it's in the air or on the ground, and its direction and speed!

JOINT JUMPING

Prairie dogs have some serious moves, such as a famous jump-yip display! They stand tall, arms out front, eyes to the skies, and STREEETCH and SQUEAK – 'EEE-eee' – all at the same time. This contagious jump gets the whole colony moving, and can be so full-on that the prairie dog falls over!

HERD HUDDLE

Elephants use all their senses to communicate. In addition to hearing, smell, and vision, they make special use of two of their sensory superpowers: the ability to feel vibrations and to use touch in their chat.

Elephant trunks have around 40,000 muscles to power them – there are only 640 muscles in the whole human body!

RUMBLE ON

Vibrations are sound waves you can feel. When those vibrations come from a sound source using very low frequencies, we often can't hear the noise but we can feel the rumble. This is called 'infrasound'. Elephants use infrasound as a long-distance call system. They send out vibrations through the ground that can be picked up by others up to 3 km (2 miles) away.

TOUCHY-FEELY

Elephant talk is big on physical contact. They touch ears, tusks, feet, tail, and trunks in their conversations. Trunks are a multi-tool communication kit. When elephants meet, they investigate each other's faces, mouths, and ears with the tip of the trunk. It's just as sensitive as human fingertips. Elephants touch each other's trunks to show friendship and trust, just like humans shake hands.

SOLE MUSIC

Elephants don't hear long-distance infrasound with their ears, they feel it through the soles of their feet! Special cells in the foot make contact with the ground to 'feel' the message. Sometimes an elephant will lift up one foot to 'hear' better. This increases the weight on the other three feet and improves contact with the ground.

23

WAKE-UP CALL

The Dawn Chorus starts about half an hour before sunrise. Spring songs are sung mostly by males to attract a mate and to deter rivals. Often, the more territorial a species, the bigger the song. Take the wren – teeny-tiny but with a voice that packs a punch. Wrens flit almost unseen in cracks and crevices but have a song to top the charts. A sing-off at dawn between two or more males is not unusual.

CALLING LONG DISTANCE

Songbirds make the very best bird-bands! They learn their songs and perform them loud and proud early each morning in spring. This breathtaking show is called the Dawn Chorus.

WINDPIPE

LUNG

SYRINX

WREN

SPECIAL SONGS

Birds 'talk' using a special voice box called a syrinx. This allows them to make two notes at once. Birds make both calls and songs. Calls are shorter, often meaning 'danger' or 'here I am'. But songs can be show-stoppers – rhythmic, rich, and demonstrating the singer's presence and strength as a mate. Each species has its own unique playlist. For example, the brown thrasher produces 2,000 different sounds and the European nightingale has around 300 complicated songs.

European chaffinches can sing an unbelievable 45 notes a second – more than any other bird!

KING PENGUIN

CALLER ID

King penguins breed in vast colonies of up to 400,000 birds. When penguin parents go to sea to fish, their chicks wander around and huddle together with thousands of identical youngsters. When the adults return, they must find their chicks in this very noisy crowd. Incredibly, every penguin has a unique identification call so they can hear and recognize each other on a beach full of baby birds squawking to be fed.

Hungry babies call frantically to find their returning mum or dad.

Penguins are often away at sea fishing for several days.

Amazingly, the parents recognize their calls among the crowd.

25

GREAT IMPRESSIONISTS

Is that the phone? Is it a plane? A motorbike? Is that a donkey in the garden? No - it's just a master bird mimic up to its old tricks.

GREATER MOUSE-EARED BAT

Greater mouse-eared bats have learned a great trick to avoid being eaten by owls. Whenever owls are spotted, the bats buzz like angry hornets. The owls flee the 'hornets' and the bats stay safe.

LYING LYREBIRDS

Complicated songs show a singer is skilled, experienced, and would make a good mate. Which is probably why a few birds have become total masters of disguise! They copy the voices of nearby birds, people, and even sounds they encounter in their environment. Superb lyrebirds are one of the world's most talented mimics. They imitate dogs barking, babies crying, chainsaws, trucks, and even car alarms!

SUPERB LYREBIRD

GUESS WHO?

When birds are hidden in trees, bird-watchers can sometimes identify them by listening to their calls. But master mimics can even fool the experts. The grey catbird is so good at copycatting, even other species fall for their tricks. They earned their name from a call that sounds like a cat's 'meow' and some even imitate local frogs.

GREY CATBIRD

NORTHERN MOCKINGBIRD

OCCUPIED!

Northern mockingbirds can copy the calls of around 200 other bird species! Scientists think that mockingbirds learn new songs to cut down competition for territory. A bird tempted to move into a desired garden will pass if the potential area seems to be packed with flocks of noisy birds. The disappointed strangers look for somewhere less busy and the mockingbirds get to keep the place all to themselves.

EUROPEAN OTTER

TURD TALK

Otter poop is black and slimy and known as spraint. Spraint is left piled in important places like stones in rivers. It is meant to be found because spraint is, basically, a smelly social media post that tells neighbours who is around. Otters add to the pile every day, so new information is being posted all the time.

DROPPING HINTS

All animals produce droppings – or poop! It's waste matter from their food. But poop is also a messaging system packed full of information about the identity of the pooper (or poopers), as well as their health and mood.

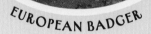

EUROPEAN BADGER

BADGER 'BATHROOM'

European badgers live in close-knit groups called clans and make their home in underground burrows called setts. Badgers guard their territories against other clans. Every badger in the group leaves droppings in just one place, called a latrine. Made on the edge of territory, and away from the sett, this super loo creates a communal scent made of the poop of all clan members. This strengthens the bonds between family members while warning other clans to keep their distance.

Poop contains DNA that scientists use to track rare species, like snow leopards.

SQUARE STACK

Wombats are loners that don't welcome strangers onto their patch. Like many species, wombats define territorial boundaries with 'poop-markers'. But unlike any other animal, each wombat dropping is cube-shaped – just like dice. This anti-roll device stops the droppings falling away from their carefully chosen poop stack – genius!

COMMON WOMBAT

AFRICAN HIPPO

SUPER SPREADERS

Pooping hippopotamuses spin their tails around frantically to scatter smelly poop in every direction. Poop splashes into the water (where these animals spend lots of time) and splatters nearby hippos. This nifty, whiffy trick marks their territory big time. Hippos have an important contact call called a 'wheeze-honk'. If an unfamiliar wheeze-honk is heard from a stranger, the hippos start turbo-pooping and tail-spinning to produce a smell that drives away intruders.

THIS IS MINE!

We mark our home – our territory – with words. There's a house name or number and an address so that people can find us. But other animals have more 'fluid' techniques. Welcome to the world of the super pee-ers!

GIANT PANDA

BUSHBABY

Bushbabies have a very good reason not to wash their hands. They deliberately pee on their hands so that everything they touch carries their scent.

TREE-MENDOUS GYMNASTICS!

Giant panda guys may look more cuddly than athletic but they're seriously good at acrobatic peeing. They reverse up a tree until they're in a handstand – then upside-down pee onto the trunk! The urine contains lots of information – including their eagerness for a mate! The wind carries the scent all around the bamboo forest, letting other pandas know.

GETTING SNIFFY!

Ever heard of 'stink-face'? That's a word used to describe the facial movements made by some animals when they sniff the air. Stink-face doesn't mean the animal is grossed out, it means it has picked up a strong scent. The funky face-pulling sends scent to an organ behind the top teeth that 'tastes' the chemical messages left in pee, poop, or sweat. It's called the 'flehmen response'.

Super-sensitive scent-detecting cells in the mouth make up the vomeronasal organ.

SPRAY-TIME

Tigers, like most cats, are big scent-talkers; they especially like to pee or 'spray' on vertical surfaces. Spray is crammed with chemicals and shouts 'this is mine!' Scientists can use this to help build up a picture of the tiger populations in an area. Spray, which is a mix of urine and gland secretions, helps them 'fingerprint' individuals using DNA.

31

SUPER SCENTS

Scent-marking is so important to some animals that they have special glands to help them in the task. Scent glands produce a sticky, smelly gloop that carries important messages to others.

TEAR-MARKED

Tiny Kirk's dik-diks are super-small African antelopes. They don't live in a herd but as a pair – one male and one female in each territory. They keep away intruders by marking every part of their habitat with a thick, waxy substance that comes from glands just below the corner of their eyes. These glands look like big, black teardrops.

KIRK'S DIK-DIK

SLOTH

Sloths are brilliant at disguise! They never need to buy deodorant because they have no scent! They sweat only from the very tip of their nose, so they smell mostly of the forest. Sloths are also covered in 'sloth moss', a green moss that makes them tough to spot in the treetops.

RING-TAILED LEMUR

SCENT SPOTS

Scent glands occur in the strangest of places! Ring-tailed lemurs have them on their wrists. Deer have them on their feet, tucked in between their 'toes' so they leave a scent-message with every step. Elephant glands are just in front of their ears, while foxes have them under their tails.

SCENT GLAND

STINK FIGHTS

Male ring-tails have 'stink fights' to determine who gets to mate. They rub their tails in scent and the smelliest wins.

FEMALE ATLAS MOTH

SINGLE-MINDED

The life of a nocturnal atlas moth is very short – around 12 weeks. They spend most of their time as caterpillars. Winged adults survive for around six days, and have one role to perform – to mate and lay eggs. Female moths produce powerful pheromones that can be blown for around 5 km (3 miles) on the wind. Male atlas moths detect the pheromones with their antennae and give chase.

MALE ATLAS
MOTH

SECRET SCENTS

Pheromones are chemicals that tell members of the same species how to act. They're some of the most powerful scents on the planet. While scent-marking with pee and poop advises those detecting the scent to respond, pheromones give an order. They're all about instinct.

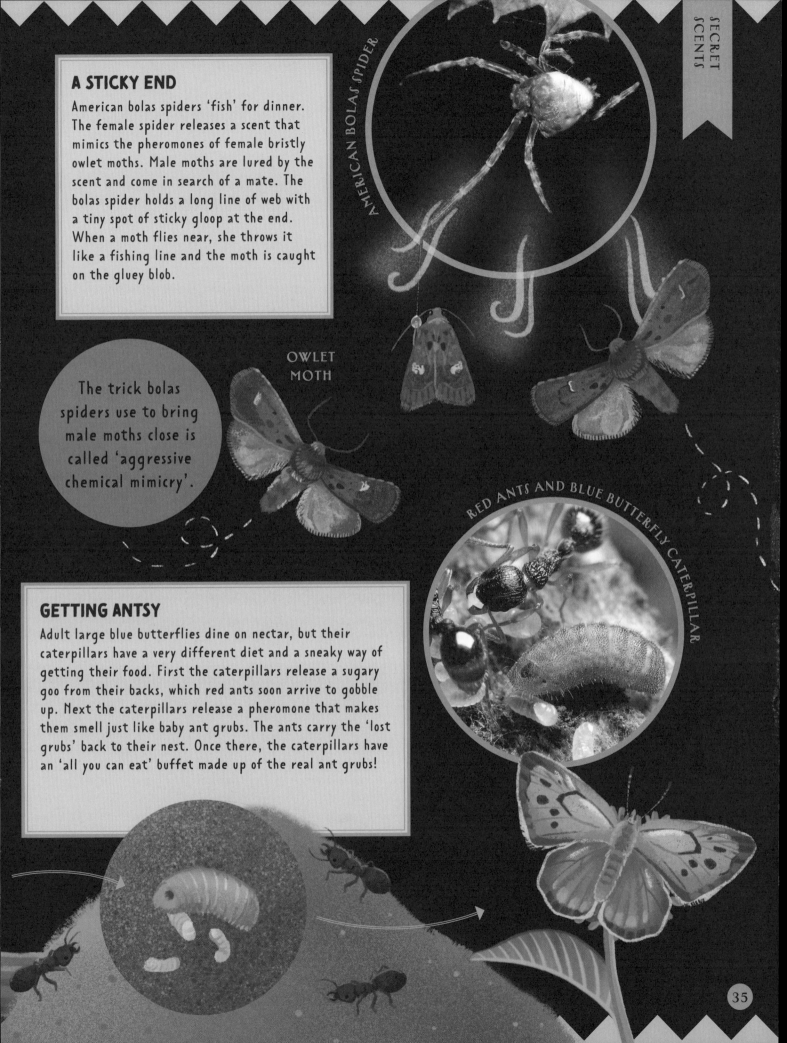

A STICKY END

American bolas spiders 'fish' for dinner. The female spider releases a scent that mimics the pheromones of female bristly owlet moths. Male moths are lured by the scent and come in search of a mate. The bolas spider holds a long line of web with a tiny spot of sticky gloop at the end. When a moth flies near, she throws it like a fishing line and the moth is caught on the gluey blob.

AMERICAN BOLAS SPIDER

The trick bolas spiders use to bring male moths close is called 'aggressive chemical mimicry'.

OWLET MOTH

RED ANTS AND BLUE BUTTERFLY CATERPILLAR

GETTING ANTSY

Adult large blue butterflies dine on nectar, but their caterpillars have a very different diet and a sneaky way of getting their food. First the caterpillars release a sugary goo from their backs, which red ants soon arrive to gobble up. Next the caterpillars release a pheromone that makes them smell just like baby ant grubs. The ants carry the 'lost grubs' back to their nest. Once there, the caterpillars have an 'all you can eat' buffet made up of the real ant grubs!

ANT ANTICS

Wood ants are super cool animals. They have a strong, highly organised social structure and almost all their communication relies on pheromones!

There are around 2½ million ants for every human on Earth. The total weight of living ants is greater than the total weight of people.

MESSAGING SYSTEM

Ants live in 'anthills', mounds of tunnels built for the colony by worker ants. Up to 400,000 wood ants can live in one nest, and they need a fast way to communicate.

Picked up on each ant's antennae, pheromones ripple through a nest in moments. They identify friends, enemies, and calls for help.

BREADCRUMB TRAILS

When ants find a great supply of food they secrete a 'trail pheromone' to mark a pathway to the feeding site that others can follow. Each ant that travels the route releases more pheromones to keep the scent strong. Which is why ants don't move in wraggle-taggle groups but in long lines following the scent of the one in front.

INFO SUPERHIGHWAY

Ants work together as a kind of super-organism. If food is scarce, pheromones tell ant grubs to stop growing, another will instruct them to grow again when food is plentiful. When an ant bites an enemy, it releases a strong pheromone that tells others to join in the attack. As an ant dies it sends out 'danger' pheromones to help keep the colony safe.

When the ants are threatened or aim to kill prey, pheromones instruct them to squirt formic acid – all together – from their abdomens.

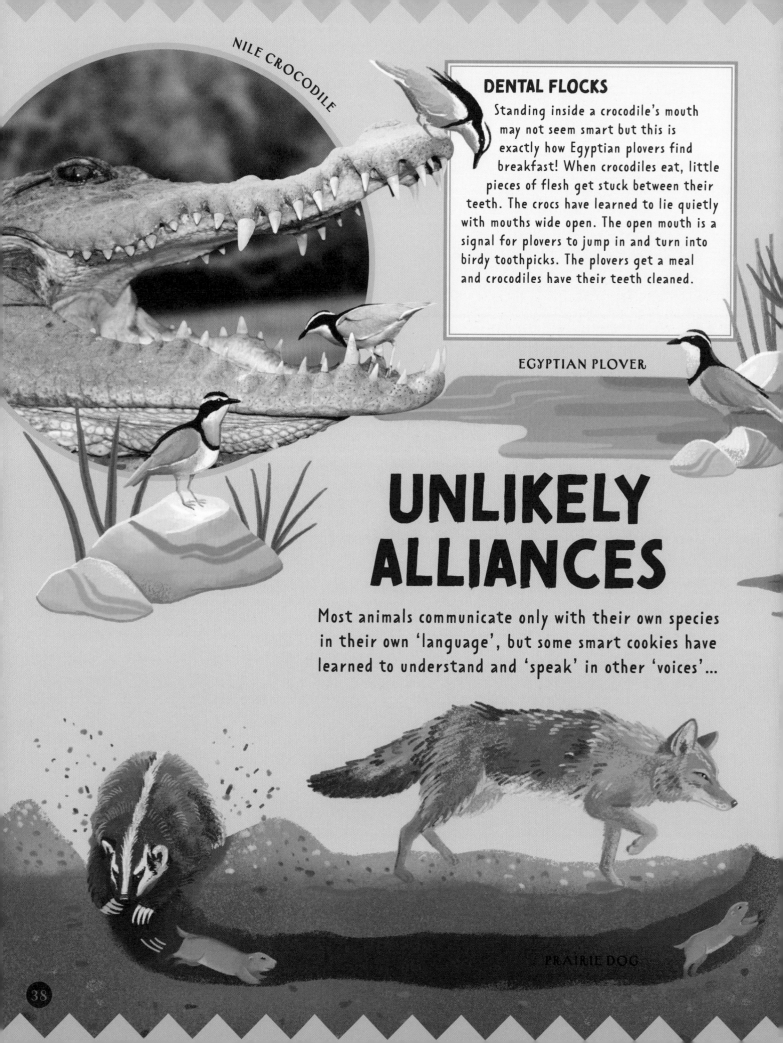

NILE CROCODILE

EGYPTIAN PLOVER

DENTAL FLOCKS

Standing inside a crocodile's mouth may not seem smart but this is exactly how Egyptian plovers find breakfast! When crocodiles eat, little pieces of flesh get stuck between their teeth. The crocs have learned to lie quietly with mouths wide open. The open mouth is a signal for plovers to jump in and turn into birdy toothpicks. The plovers get a meal and crocodiles have their teeth cleaned.

UNLIKELY ALLIANCES

Most animals communicate only with their own species in their own 'language', but some smart cookies have learned to understand and 'speak' in other 'voices'...

PRAIRIE DOG

BLUESTREAK
CLEANER WRASSE

SPA DAY

Bluestreak cleaner wrasse are fish that offer up spa services where much bigger, predatory fish clients – including sharks – can stop by for a spruce-up. These fearless cleaners nibble away sea lice and dead scales from clients. To make clear their intentions, the wrasse perform a funky dance while the client fish stops all movement. These signals mean both parties recognize a deal has been done.

COYOTE

AMERICAN BADGER

FIERCE FRIENDS

Adult prairie dogs are fast. They can run, turn quickly, and then suddenly disappear underground. Hungry coyotes and American badgers sometimes join forces to hunt them. These species work together to cover all bases. If prairie dogs run, the fast-moving coyote chases; if the dogs dive underground, the badger has no problem digging them up. We don't yet know how the pair decide to hunt together.

RAVEN WING

Despite not having hands primed for pointing, ravens use their wings and long beaks to point out sources of food or danger. It takes a human baby almost a whole year to figure out how to use this skill. Ravens can also learn to count, are sharp at maths, and can use tools to solve problems.

BIRD SUPER-BRAINS

Ravens and their close relatives, magpies and crows, are so smart that they ace tests usually only passed by primates – including humans! Ravens are great 'gesturers': they can show each other, and other species, exactly where they need to look!

COMMON RAVEN

TIMBER WOLF

ODD COUPLE

Ravens often follow hunting wolves and feed on their leftovers. Some ravens form such close bonds with wolf cubs that they play fetch or tug-of-war with branches.

In the language of the Inuit who live in the Arctic, ravens are known as 'wolf-birds'.

CALLING THE WOLVES

When ravens spot an animal that has died naturally, they have a problem. Their beaks are not strong enough to break into the tough carcass. They need a little help from the wolves. The hungry ravens 'cronk' loudly and fly above the meal to call the pack.

The wolves tear open the body so they and the ravens can dine together.

PLAY FAIR

Ravens expect their friends to play by the rules! If they share the best food, the flock will welcome them and invite them to join in their noisy play flights. If ravens don't share and keep the best snacks to themselves, they'll be ignored. Ravens can also recognize and remember human faces. When people who have hurt them show up, the birds call out to warn other ravens about the danger.

41

TOAD-ALLY IMPRESSIVE

Snakes swallow their food whole. They're skilled at judging the maximum size of their dinner. So if small animals can somehow make themselves look bigger, a snake might not see them as prey. Some smart common toads have figured this out. If a snake is spotted, these toads stretch onto their tippy-toes and become three times taller. A kind of 'swallow me if you can' gesture!

GUINEAFOWL PUFFERFISH

PUFFED UP

Guineafowl pufferfish live in tropical waters. They are clumsy swimmers – risky for fish hunted by hungry tiger sharks. But pufferfish make themselves look too big to eat by swallowing huge amounts of water. In less than 15 seconds, the pufferfish swells up like a giant balloon. They are as round as a beach ball and just as hard to swallow – even for a shark!

Bluffing about your true size and scariness is called 'deimatic behaviour'.

LYING FOR A LIVING

Size matters! Relative size is one way of working out who is likely to survive in any confrontation. Some species have cunning methods of making themselves look much bigger than they really are.

HAIR-RAISING!

Chimpanzees squabble a lot, but most cool down quickly. There is no mistaking when chimps are genuinely frightened or angry – their hair stands on end! This is called 'piloerection' and makes the chimp look huge. Other chimps recognize this as a sign of real anger. Piloerection happens when tiny muscles in the skin tighten. Exactly the same effect occurs in humans – we call it 'goosebumps'.

INDIAN COBRA

CHIMPANZEE

EXTRA EYES

Indian or spectacled cobras have venomous bites that can kill humans. But 'wasting' venom on someone too big to swallow is pointless. Instead, the cobra tries to persuade larger adversaries to move on. Cobras have loose skin on the sides of the head that can open into a wide hood. It signals: "I'm big – don't mess with me". A cobra that is hooded, hissing, and rearing up isn't angry – it's afraid. The back of the hood also shows huge false 'eyes', which add to the display.

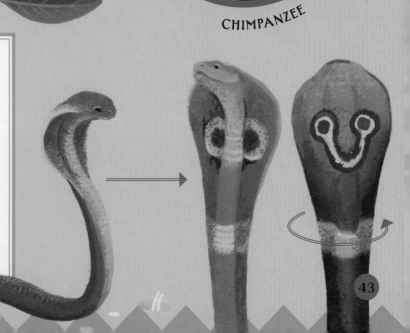

TRICKY BEHAVIOUR

Animals have inventive ways to find food and stay safe – some are downright dishonest. People often say that animals never lie, but the truth is they fib – all the time!

FORK-TAILED DRONGO

WARNING!

Fork-tailed drongos are super-smart birds that often live close to meerkats in the Kalahari Desert. Both species have learned to recognize each other's alarm calls. This call is a warning that a dangerous predator is near, so it's time to hide.

LIARS AND THIEVES

Sometimes, when meerkats dig up particularly juicy grubs that the birds think look tasty, the drongos give a false alarm call, pretending danger is close by. The meerkats dash underground and the drongos swoop down and steal the grubs! Drongos can mimic over 50 alarm calls, including the meerkats' own!

BABOON

When baby baboons are scolded by Mum, they sometimes give the alarm call that means: 'Danger!' Mum falls for the trick just once before realizing their baby is telling lies!

STRIATED HERON

FISH BAIT!

About 80 years ago, a striated heron was seen collecting bread from garden bird tables. These herons were known to eat small fish and frogs but not bread – strange! Local bird watchers turned detective to solve the mystery. They followed the heron and spotted the bird dropping the bread into a lake. The fish in the lake started to nibble on the bread, and the heron darted forward, grabbed a fish, and swallowed it. Thousands of striated herons have now learned this trick.

EASTERN CORAL SNAKE

LOOK OUT!

Some species send out messages claiming to be super harmful if eaten, when in reality, it's just a trick and they're totally harmless!

SCARLET KINGSNAKE

DANGER!

Eastern coral snakes have a wickedly venomous bite. To advertise to predators that they're dangerous and bad to eat, their skin is striped brightly. The jazzy red, yellow, and black colouring is a warning. This type of signalling is called 'aposematism'.

FOOLED YOU

The scarlet kingsnake is non-venomous but has a pattern of stripes or rings similar to the Eastern coral snake. The kingsnake is basically wearing the 'clothes' of a much more dangerous snake. This bluffing is called 'Batesian mimicry'.

SEQUENCING...

Look closely at both snakes and you'll notice that their colours repeat in a different order. Both species live side by side in parts of North America, and local people are taught to remember a simple sentence ID-ing the snakes to keep them safe: "Red on yellow, kill a fellow; red on black, venom lack".

EASTERN CORAL SNAKE

SCARLET KINGSNAKE

BLOOMING AMAZING

The awesome female orchid mantis is brilliant at disguise. She uses a trick that is the opposite of Batesian mimicry. She pretends to be harmless when she's actually really dangerous. The mantis is a predator that seems to be a flower. She invites insects to sip her nectar before snapping them up at lightning speed!

The mantis has a super-fast strike!

ORCHID MANTIS

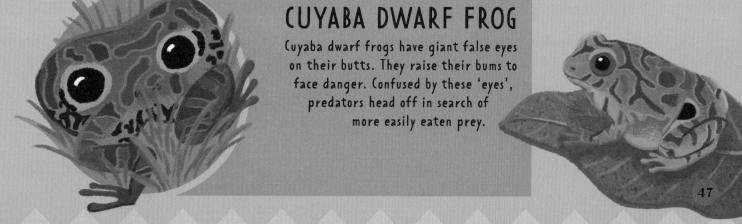

CUYABA DWARF FROG

Cuyaba dwarf frogs have giant false eyes on their butts. They raise their bums to face danger. Confused by these 'eyes', predators head off in search of more easily eaten prey.

47

Vultures take up a high vantage point to give themselves a good view of food opportunities.

TURKEY VULTURE

MIXED MESSAGES

Turkey vultures feast on the flesh of dead animals. Sadly for them, their reputation can signal to other animals that there is easy food around. To discourage other predators from muscling in, these super-pukers have a truly gross way of distracting their enemies while also making themselves less appetizing as tasty grub.

CARCASS CATCHER

The vulture is a supreme scavenger. It soars high in the sky, casting an eye all around in the hope it will spot the corpse of another animal. Once located, the vulture swoops down to tuck into the bits of flesh still left on the poor dead creature's body.

SEA HARE

This seemingly defenceless creature uses a cunning ploy to evade predators. When threatened, the sea hare releases a cloud of ink. This confuses and conceals it from its foe, but scientists have discovered it may also disrupt a predator's sense of smell, making the sea hare seem less appetizing.

SICK TRICK

Tucking into a dead animal might seem risk-free at first, but there are always prowling predators lurking. Sensing another animal close by, the vulture projectile vomits onto them. The stinky puke can seem quite yum to this distracted foe. Not wasting any time, the vulture makes a hasty getaway and flies away to safety!

49

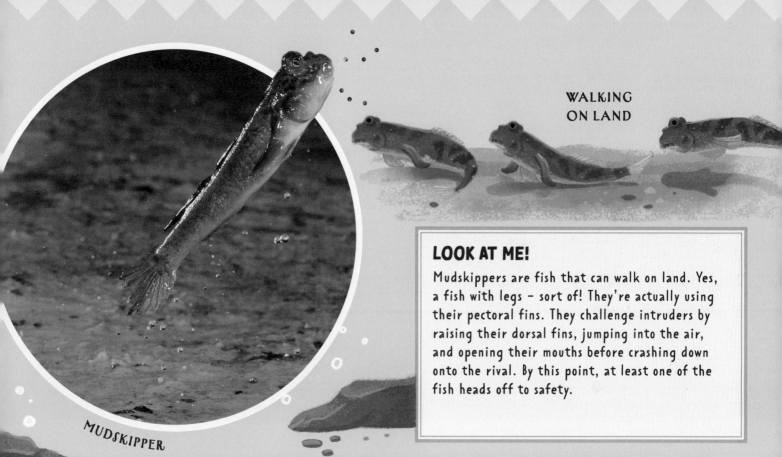

MUDSKIPPER

LOOK AT ME!

Mudskippers are fish that can walk on land. Yes, a fish with legs – sort of! They're actually using their pectoral fins. They challenge intruders by raising their dorsal fins, jumping into the air, and opening their mouths before crashing down onto the rival. By this point, at least one of the fish heads off to safety.

SHOWS OF STRENGTH

For wild animals, even a small injury can result in death. As a result, many species have worked out it's better to settle arguments with shows of strength where none of them are actually injured.

KISSING GOURAMI

PUCKER UP

Kissing gourami – kisser fish – may look cute as they smooch together, but the kiss is really a show of strength between two males. They lock mouths and each tries to roll the other, like a kind of arm-wrestle but with lips! This lets them guess the strength of their rival.

BAD HAIR DAY

Red deer roar at the beginning of the breeding season – or rut – to tell rivals that this place is taken. Stags size up each other's antlers to see whose are the largest and strongest. To make their antlers look more awesome, the stags sometimes head-butt undergrowth to get the antlers covered in vegetation. These snazzy antler-accessories can be enough to persuade rivals to back away.

American green frogs judge each other by the pitch of their croaks. Small frogs produce higher notes, but some tiny frogs have learned to croak more deeply to increase their status.

RED DEER

ORIENTAL RAT SNAKES

GET KNOTTED

Male oriental rat snakes establish who owns territory by a kind of ritualized dance where they intertwine with each other, like plaiting strings or trying to tie a knot! The rivals dance until the loser realizes he's outclassed and slithers away.

BOING-BOING

Springboks are top athletes! Their name means 'jumping antelope' in Afrikaans. When threatened, they 'pronk' – leap high in the air to prove they are too strong and fast to catch. The whole herd yo-yo up and down if a predator is close. Pronk is the Afrikaans word for 'show off'.

SPRINGBOK

LION

NOT ME!

A single springbok pronk says: "I'm fit". But when a whole group of springboks use the same display strategy, it helps predators work out which individuals are weakest in the herd. Then they'll target the least strong and able.

YOU CAN'T CATCH ME

Some shows of agility are signals that tell other animals that they are super healthy and aren't worth chasing. Fit, fast animals make bad prey!

PUSH-UP CHALLENGE

Western fence lizards do energetic push-ups in easy-to-see places to show they're strong and fit. Their bright blue sides seem to flash with each press-up to impress mates or rivals. When another male lizard arrives to strut his push-up stuff, they both become super-charged, flashing away to show who's boss!

WESTERN FENCE LIZARD

HIPPOPOTAMUS

Hippos' yawns might seem to make them look tired, but there's nothing sleepy about them – it's a yawning warning! Their gape is all about displaying huge teeth and reminding others not to start an argument.

53

BACK OFF!

Some animals are masters at saying: "watch out for me!" Threat displays become more obvious and insistent as dangers move closer, so animals need their 'stay back' message to be understood.

Rattlers rattle more quickly as a threat gets closer.

EARLY-WARNING SYSTEM

The rattle of a Western diamondback rattlesnake can easily be mistaken as a signal they are about to strike. But rattlers are actually rattling politely to warn predators not to get too close. It's basically a way of stopping an injury before it can happen.

CLICKY-CLACKERS

The rattle is made by a series of connected hollow scales at the tip of the tail. They are shaken together like maracas and make a 'ch-ch' sound. The rattle-scales are made of keratin, just like human fingernails. Adult rattlers can shake their tail 90 times a second. Some scientists believe the rattle originated to stop bison stepping on snakes camouflaged in the grass.

OUCH!

Rattlers bite around 1,000 people every year in North America. More than half of those bites occur when people are trying to handle snakes; others happen when snakes are surprised. Less than four people each year die from its bite.

WESTERN DIAMONDBACK RATTLESNAKE

BEAVER

Beaver tails are genius multi-tools. They act as a counterbalance when gnawing trees, a fat store for winter, and as an alarm system! If a beaver sees danger, it slaps its tail hard onto the water, producing a loud crack that echoes around the lake. This is a signal for the other beavers to hide. It also tells predators they've been spotted!

55

SEEING RED!

Red is a special colour in the natural world. Vivid and bright, some animals use it to shriek: "Look out! I'm super bad to eat!". This colour-warning is called 'aposematism'.

RED OR DEAD

Red is nature's most common warning colour. It stands out well against green vegetation and still looks sharp at a distance. Just like some road signs, red is used because it provides contrast to the environment. Predators learn, over time, that a species of a particular colour does not make for a good meal and could mean pain, discomfort, or even death.

PANAMANIAN GOLDEN TORTOISE BEETLE

TOMATO FROG

Tomato frogs live on the island of Madagascar. If a predator tries one for lunch, the frog puffs up his body and releases a white, gross-tasting liquid from its skin. This numbs the predator's mouth and tongue and the frog is usually dropped unharmed. The lesson for snacky predators? Never - ever - eat bright red frogs!

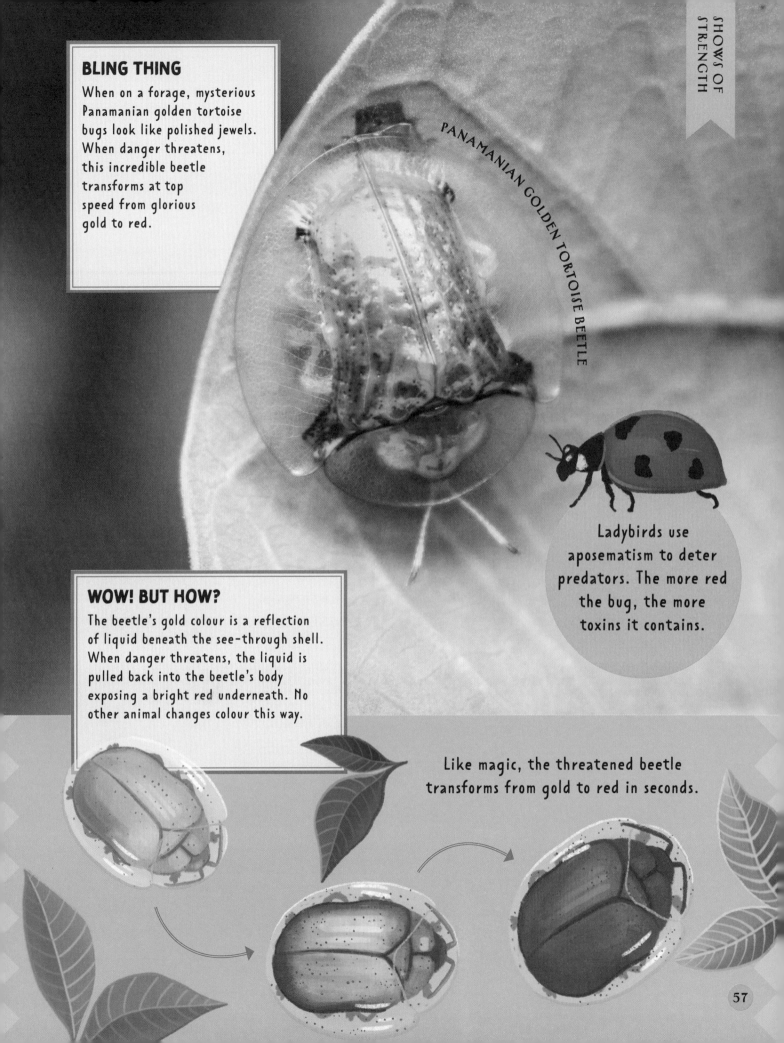

BLING THING

When on a forage, mysterious Panamanian golden tortoise bugs look like polished jewels. When danger threatens, this incredible beetle transforms at top speed from glorious gold to red.

PANAMANIAN GOLDEN TORTOISE BEETLE

Ladybirds use aposematism to deter predators. The more red the bug, the more toxins it contains.

WOW! BUT HOW?

The beetle's gold colour is a reflection of liquid beneath the see-through shell. When danger threatens, the liquid is pulled back into the beetle's body exposing a bright red underneath. No other animal changes colour this way.

Like magic, the threatened beetle transforms from gold to red in seconds.

57

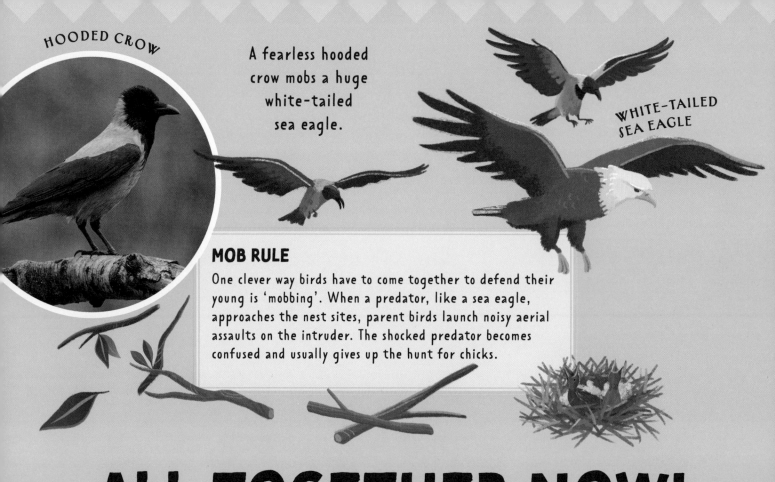

HOODED CROW

A fearless hooded crow mobs a huge white-tailed sea eagle.

WHITE-TAILED SEA EAGLE

MOB RULE

One clever way birds have to come together to defend their young is 'mobbing'. When a predator, like a sea eagle, approaches the nest sites, parent birds launch noisy aerial assaults on the intruder. The shocked predator becomes confused and usually gives up the hunt for chicks.

ALL TOGETHER NOW!

Some astonishing animal comms are more about group conversations than one-on-one defence. Strength in numbers means smaller birds have a fast and effective way to challenge enemies.

SPARROWHAWK

CALL TO ARMS

Lots of different species come together to harass the predator. The frantic birds give special mobbing calls to draw attention to the frenzy and encourage more to join in.

Mobbing is an example of 'mutualism' - birds working together to protect chicks of the whole mob.

ARCTIC TERN

YUCK!

Mobbing can include dive-bombing, ear-splitting squawks, and even pooping or vomiting on intruders! Birds that breed in colonies – like terns or gulls – are especially skilled at mobbing. Other top mobsters include crows and songbirds.

ARCTIC FOX

AMERICAN CROW

BALTIMORE ORIOLE

WHO GETS IT?

Which species birds come to see as a threat depends on the danger they pose. Songbirds, such as the Baltimore oriole, see crows as dangerous, while crows see hawks or owls as menaces. Some mobs will tackle intruding mammals – like foxes, snakes, or even people.

HERRING GULL

STOP THIEF!

Gulls scavenging on the beach will sometimes mob to nab treats from humans. Ice creams are popular targets. The mob distract the eater of the snack for just long enough for a zoomy gull to dive in and snatch!

Bison use lots of grunts to stay in touch with each other. We call these 'contact calls'. They reassure the herd that everything is fine.

DEMOCRACY

Just like most countries and committees vote in leadership contests, bison make decisions based on the 'majority rule'.

BODY LANGUAGE

Bison 'cast a vote' to move in a particular direction by positioning their bodies in a certain way. Some members of the herd might fancy a spot of lush grazing to the north, while others might prefer to head east to an especially good waterhole. Bison point their bodies in the direction they prefer.

VOTE NOW!

European bison, also called wisent, use lots of vocalizations. When they're upset or when males are in the mood to mate, they growl! But chatty bison also have the ability to 'vote with their feet' when deciding where to go!

ZZZAP!

Scientists are using the bison's follow-my-leader behaviour to try to limit conflicts between bison and farmers. Likely bison leaders are fitted with a collar that triggers mild electric shocks if they raid crops. By persuading one bison to head away, they persuade the whole herd.

BISON WEARING SHOCK COLLAR

Bison vote for their preferred direction of travel using their body like a compass pointer.

FOLLOW ME

Eventually, one individual will make a move towards a chosen location and some of the herd will follow. Sometimes the herd splits for a while, but more often all will go in the direction preferred by the majority of followers. This collective decision-making is unusual in the world of animals.

61

FLIGHT TIME

Migration is a mysterious and pretty miraculous process that takes animals on epic journeys across the world. Science is only just beginning to understand how some of the decisions about when to leave are made.

BARN SWALLOW

SOLO TRIPS

Some migrations – like swallows shifting between Europe and Africa – are instinctive. The birds move from breeding grounds to wintering grounds as individuals, and they know where to go and how to get there without guidance from parents. Others, like Canada geese, are different...

GOING GETS TOUGH

Canada geese decide to leave their summer range when food becomes scarce and the weather turns cold. But they don't simply leave; instead, they 'talk' with each other to signal that they're ready to head off. The geese start to honk loudly and to sky-point – to point their beaks straight up to the sky. Single families or groups of families head south together.

Sociable geese display noisily to show each other that they're ready to move on together.

NEW FLIERS

Canada geese don't navigate by instinct but by experience. They have to LEARN to find their way. They learn to recognize landmarks – like coastlines and mountains. They may also use the Sun and stars to help them stay on track. Young geese rely on parent and adult birds to guide them so they need to stick together.

CANADA GEESE

SAVING ENERGY

Travelling as a flock has a great number of advantages for the geese. Flying takes lots of energy, so to make the journey less tough, they fly in calm weather and with a tailwind. They also fly in formation – this reduces wind 'drag' on all but the lead bird and gives them a little extra lift.

Chevron or V-formation flying uses 'slip-streaming' to save energy.

HELLO HELLO

Wandering albatrosses mate for life and are serious romantics. After their young have flown, they head out to sea alone for many months. When they reunite, the excited pair shares a noisy welcome dance. They spread their huge wings, tap beaks, and shake their heads – all while making very loud noises. Not the most pleasing sound to human ears but it definitely works for the albatross!

ROADRUNNER

Chocolates? Not for roadrunners! Their top-ranking love token is freshly killed lizard!

MOVERS AND SHAKERS

Birds do all kinds of things in springtime ahead of raising chicks. This is the time for courtship and wooing, for building bonds and trust. Bird dates are all about gift-giving, having the right moves, and showing off with ritual dances.

GENTOO PENGUINS

ROCK MUSIC

Forget flowers, nothing says 'I love you' in gentoo penguin like a nice pebble or two! Gentoo penguins nest on rocky towers of stones. The penguins collect the best stones from the shoreline and present them to their mates while making gentle chuckling sounds. These 'prized gifts' are added to the nest. The cheeky penguins also steal stones from the nests of neighbours – who steal them right back!

FEMALE SATIN BOWERBIRD

MALE SATIN BOWERBIRD

SHOW HOME

Arty male satin bowerbirds make the most stylish homes. They build a dome of grass that's decorated with treasures stolen from town. Most prized are petals, pebbles, bottle-tops, plastic forks, snail-shells, drinking straws – anything colourful and bright. These are carefully placed around the 'bower' – or home – to woo passing females. Some bowerbirds choose decorations of many colours, but most pick just blues.

GREAT CRESTED GREBES

MAKE LIKE A PENGUIN

The great crested grebe's 'penguin dance' is all about high-speed water-running, head-shaking, and waterweeds! It begins with males and females calling to each other across a lake. They nod heads before diving underwater to collect weeds. Carrying the weeds in their beaks, they swim towards each other, paddling madly and rising high in the water until they are almost upright. Eventually, they touch chests and the dance is done. The two are now together!

A COURTSHIP SPECTACLE

The male Vogelkop superb bird-of-paradise puts on quite a show. With the female watching on, the male raises his wings to form a hood and then bounces, darts forwards, backwards, and side to side around the female, all in the hope she will be impressed enough that she will allow him to mate with her.

DATING DISCO

For these animals, attracting a mate all comes down to how well they can perform on the dance floor. These creative creatures try to woo their mate with dance moves and routines in the hope they will receive a perfect score from the judges!

PEACOCK SPIDER

DANCE FOR YOUR LIFE!

This colourful critter is about the size of a grain of rice. Luckily, the male peacock spider has some attention-grabbing tricks up his sleeve. Once he has a female's attention, he raises his colourful body and back legs and shimmies from side to side. This mating dance needs to be impressive or the bigger female might decide the male is better as a meal than a mate!

Unlike most animals, male weedy seadragons are responsible for carrying the eggs of their young.

WEEDY SEADRAGONS

SYNCHRONIZED SWIMMERS

Male and female weedy seadragons have an especially enchanting mating ritual. They glide gracefully together, side by side in perfect harmony, mirroring each other's body movements. This elegant, slow dance typically starts as the spring evening light begins to fade and carries on long into the night.

SEDUCTION DANCE

This bizarre dance sees the male ostrich bend his legs, stoop down, and extend his wings to fully display his feathers before rhythmically swaying from side to side. The elegance of his display will ultimately be judged by the female as she decides whether his attempts to impress her are good enough.

OSTRICH

WHO'S BOSS?

When trouble threatens, friends and rivals need to know who is in charge, who is dangerous, and who can be trusted. Monkeys are particularly known for this.

SHAKING BRANCHES

BRANCH MANAGER

Barbary macaques live in troops with a very strict hierarchy. Much of their comms works to maintain this hierarchy – especially when competing for food or mates. Macaques 'talk' using sounds and body language. When arguments get heated, the leading male macaques climb a tree and shake the branches. The male that moves the biggest branch is the winner.

BOSSY

Threat displays are much safer for everyone than actual fights. So dominant macaques use facial expressions to show their mood, as if to say "don't mess with me".

SO SORRY

Other macaques work hard to show they pose no threat. They adopt a submissive expression that shows fear and distress. It means they're not about to challenge the leaders.

MAKING UP

When fights do break out it's important that the troop work to fix the tension. One of the best ways to do this is to groom each other or to share a hug.

WHITE-FACED CAPUCHIN

When white-faced capuchins are threatened, they have a very cool defence. Two monkeys put their heads together, one above the other. Both monkeys stare wildly and snarl to show their long teeth. Pesky predators see a bigger head and far more teeth than they expected and make a quick exit!

BARBARY MACAQUES

TOUCH

Group grooming is a super-important communication tool for the monkeys. It has nothing to do with keeping clean and everything to do with building friendships.

Macaques engage in social or mutual grooming for hours every day.

69

BLINK BLINK

Flickering fireflies are beetles that know how to get noticed after dark. Just like a torch, fireflies send out light signals by flashing their abdomens on and off. This is how males attract a mate. With so many different species of firefly, each species has its own code – a unique flash pattern – to make sure they only attract their own species.

Bioluminescence is produced when a chemical called luciferin in an animal's body reacts with oxygen.

HUMPBACK ANGLERFISH

DEATH STARE

Female humpback anglerfish have a deadly grin full of needle-sharp teeth. Anglerfish lure their prey close with long, thin rods that grow from between their eyes. The tip of the rod glows in the darkness and attracts small fish to the giant mouth. Snap! The jaws close and the anglerfish swallows her dinner.

COOL INVITATIONS

In the dark of a moonless night or deep beneath the surface of the ocean, some flashy creatures signal using light itself; they are brilliantly bioluminescent.

DINOFLAGELLATES

OUT OF THE BLUE

Dinoflagellates are strange little creatures that are neither plant nor animal, but something in between! They are so small they can only be seen through a microscope. Dinoflagellates live in the ocean, and at night, millions of them rise to the surface, making huge areas of the sea light up with twinkling, blue sparkles. Science isn't yet sure why this happens.

FLASHLIGHT FISH

SCHOOLING TOGETHER

Mysterious flashlight fish are tiny synchronized swimmers who hunt together in huge 'schools'. They coordinate their swim positions by sight, and bring along their own light to help them see in the dark. The light is made in a pouch beneath the fishes' eye. The pouch is home to friendly bioluminescent bacteria, which glow, but can be dimmed by the fish covering the pouch. The schools make complex movements, as though they have minds of their own.

DINING OUT

Imagine you get the BIGGEST birthday cake ever. Do you eat it yourself or do you share? Some very special animals share food to make sure that others have enough to eat...

FINDING NECTAR

When a hungry honeybee finds a patch of flowers with rich nectar, she flies back to the hive and tells the other bees how to find it.

ABDOMEN

HONEYBEE

DINNER DANCE

Bees don't draw a treasure map, instead they dance directions to the flowers! This is the waggle dance. The bee turns this way and that in a figure-of-eight.

FOLLOWING INSTRUCTION

Using the Sun and hive as markers, the bees follow her coded instructions.

BAT CHAT

Vampire bats are bloodthirsty! Their diet is 100 per cent blood! They live in roosts in hard-to-reach places like deep caves and hollow trees in Mexico, and Central and South America. We're only just beginning to understand how complex their 'talk' can be. Bats have 'friends' and 'allies', they have special calls that mean 'I'm lonely' and others that mean 'stay away'.

If a roost-mate is hungry, female bats will spit up blood into the mouth of friends.

VAMPIRE BAT

DINNER, DINNER

When the bats are full up, they use an ultrasonic sound to call their friends to the feast. The bat's 'guest' is usually a roost-mate! An open wound means a faster meal for the guest.

SPINE TINGLING

When the night is at its darkest, bats leave their roosts to hunt. They seek out a host to feed from – cattle are a favourite. They land on the animal and use their heat-seeking noses to locate a vein. Their razor-sharp teeth scrape deep into the skin and the bats lap up their meal. Bats can bite people – but do so only very rarely!

73

LET'S 'SPEAK' HUMAN!

How would it be if we could REALLY talk with the animals? Some super-smart species have learned to 'talk' and understand 'human speak'.

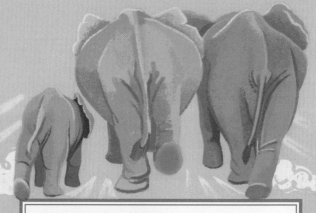

FRIEND OR FOE?

Some African elephants have learned to recognize the local hunters' language. If elephants hear locals speaking a language not used by hunters, they stay still. But a few words of hunter language and the elephants make a swift exit.

KOKO THE GORILLA

AFRICAN ELEPHANT

APE EMOTIONS

Koko, a lowland gorilla, became part of a study in ape communication. Koko was taught Gorilla Sign Language, where words are made with hand gestures. She signed more than 1,000 words and understood around 2,000 spoken words according to her caregivers. When Koko's cat friend died, she signed "cry", "sad", and "frown". The same kinds of emotions humans feel if we lose a friend.

LOVE

TICKLE

HUNGRY

74

ALEX THE PARROT

PRETTY SMART BOY!

Alex the African grey parrot did so much more than mimic human speech – he understood it! Part of a 30-year scientific study, he learned to use 100 words, could figure out basic maths, and identify different shapes and colours. Like a young child, he was able to use "no" to refuse things he didn't want to do and "want" to ask for things he liked.

Alex died peacefully. His last words to his carer were: "You be good. I love you".

BORDER COLLIE HERDING SHEEP

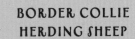

SEARCH AND RESCUE DOG

TALKIES!

Whether it's the Great Dane or Chihuahua, all dogs are a descendant of wild wolves. They've been living and working alongside humans for 25,000 years and know so much more than 'sit' and 'stay'. These super-smart pooches work as sheepdogs, in rescue, detection, and protection. Studies and brain scans show most pet pups understand around 90 human words – similar to an 18-month-old baby – but some know more than 200! They also read our body language and mood. And the smartest breed of dog? It's the border collie.

STRIKING A BARGAIN

Sometimes finding food involves nothing more than sharing a common goal and knowing the right 'people'.

SWEET TALK

Greater honeyguides eat the wax and grubs found inside wild bee nests, but need help to break the nest open. Humans love bees' honey but can't always find the nests. By working together, both sides can benefit. Incredibly, in Mozambique, birds and humans have been doing just that for thousands of years!

GREATER HONEYGUIDE

A HONEY-HUNT

It all hinges on teamwork. The humans make a 'brrr-hmm' sound that lets the honeyguides know they're off on a honey-hunt. They carry axes to open the nests and fire to subdue the bees. The birds join them and, using their own chattering 'tya' calls, lead the hunters to nearby nests. The humans harvest the honey, leaving the beeswax for the honeyguides.

Humans call to the honeyguides at the start of the honey hunt.

Honeyguides lead the hunters to the bees' nest and both eat their fill.

MONKEYING AROUND

Uluwatu Temple in Bali, Indonesia, is a favourite tourist destination and home to a troop of long-tailed macaques. Legend says that the monkeys are the souls of warriors who protect the temple. They are believed to bring happiness – but they also bring their own special brand of fun and games.

LONG-TAILED MACAQUE

Cross-species comms change as animals learn and adapt to new opportunities.

SWAPSIES

These plucky primates have learned a cunning trick! They grab a tourist's phone and offer it back, only to snatch it away again. There's no trade unless the tourists offer food in exchange! The macaques have learned to steal high-value items – like sunglasses and wallets – in the trade-off for treats! Once the humans understand the deal, everyone is happy!

INDEX

ABOUT THE AUTHORS

As a child MICHAEL LEACH's dream job was to visit remote lands and talk with the wild animals he found. His school's career advisor shook her head in despair until Michael decided to become a zoologist and film-maker. Later, as a BBC camera operator, wildlife photographer, and author, he finally got to meet the chimps, macaques, and snow monkeys he'd studied. He's now an honorary member of a troop of mountain gorillas! Michael loves chocolate, adventures, and exploring.

MERIEL LLAND was raised with a family of rescued geese, funky pigeons, hissy cats, grumpy dogs, and one very smart piglet. She spent way too much time learning to 'speak' chicken! A writer, photographer, and film-poet, Meriel is passionate about conservation and protecting the planet.

Meriel and Michael write, give talks, undertake expeditions and photo-shoots to share their wonder in the natural world. Together they have written more than 40 books.

ABOUT THE ILLUSTRATOR

ASIA ORLANDO is a digital artist, illustrator, and environmentalist. Asia creates artwork for books, magazines, products, and posters. Her work focuses on harmony between animals, humans, and the environment. She's also the founder of Our Planet Week, a social media event for illustrators aimed to address environmental issues.

ACKNOWLEDGMENTS

The publisher would like to thank the following for their kind permission to reproduce their photographs:

(Key: a-above; b-below/bottom; c-centre; f-far; l-left; r-right; t-top)

6 Alamy Stock Photo: mauritius images GmbH / Gerard Lacz (tl); Thomas Marent / Minden Pictures (cr). **Dreamstime.com:** Jonathan Oberholster (bc). **7 Alamy Stock Photo:** Mark Bowler (cr); Sorin Colac (tl). **8 Alamy Stock Photo:** STERKL (tl); Quang Nguyen Vinh (crb). **9 Alamy Stock Photo:** Victor Tyakht (tr). **Hctor Bottai:** (bl). **10-11 Alamy Stock Photo:** Robertharding / Christian Kober (t). **12 Alamy Stock Photo:** Blickwinkel / F. Hecker. **14 Alamy Stock Photo:** Nature Picture Library / Mark MacEwen (r). **15 naturepl. com:** Chien Lee (t). **16-17 Alamy Stock Photo:** Nature Picture Library / Tony Wu (t). **18 Alamy Stock Photo:** Konrad Wothe / Minden Pictures (br). **Dreamstime.com:** Ruslan Gilmanshin (cla). **19 Alamy Stock Photo:** imageBROKER / Herbert Kehrer (cr). Dreamstime.com: Anagram1 (tr). **20-21 naturepl.com:** Donald M. Jones (t). **22 Alamy Stock Photo:** John Warburton-Lee Photography / Nigel Pavitt (c). **23 Alamy Stock Photo:** Jamie Pham (t). **24 Getty Images / iStock:** Andrew_Howe (r). **25 Alamy Stock Photo:** Robertharding / Michael Nolan (t). **26 Alamy Stock Photo:** Blickwinkel / Hauke (b). **27 Alamy Stock Photo:** AGAMI Photo Agency / Brian E. Small (c); William Leaman (bl). **28 Alamy Stock Photo:** Colin Black (clb); Fabrice Bettex Photography (tl). **29 Alamy Stock Photo:** AfriPics.com (cl); Dave Watts (cra). **30 naturepl.com:** Suzi Eszterhas (c). **31 naturepl.com:** Andy Rouse (c). **32 Alamy Stock Photo:** Malcolm Schuyl (c). **33 Dreamstime.com:** Andrey Gudkov (ca); Emanuele Leoni (l). **34 Alamy Stock Photo:** Nature Picture Library / Ingo Arndt (tl). **35 Judy Gallagher:** (tr). **T. Komatsu / Japan. Sci Rep 6, 36364 (2016). 36-37 Alamy Stock Photo:** Nature Picture Library / Kim Taylor (c). **38 Warren Photographic Limited:** (tl). **39 Alamy Stock Photo:** Helmut Corneli (cla/ca); Konrad Wothe / Minden Pictures (bl); Donald M. Jones / Minden Pictures (br). **40 Dreamstime.com:** Mikalay Varabey (tl). **40-41 Alamy Stock Photo:** Danita Delimont Creative / Danita Delimont. **41 Dreamstime.com:** Mikalay Varabey (bl). **42 Alamy Stock Photo:** Mike Lane (tr); Fred Bavendam / Minden Pictures (cl). **43 Alamy Stock Photo:** Dinodia Photos RM (cl). **naturepl.com:** Ernie Janes (cr). **44 Alamy Stock Photo:** Ann and Steve Toon (l). **45 123RF.com:** gator (t). **46 Alamy Stock Photo:** Robert Hamilton (c). **naturepl.com:** MYN / Paul Marcellini (tl). **47 Alamy Stock Photo:** Nature Picture Library / Alex Hyde (c). **48-49 Alamy Stock Photo:** Tom Vezo / Minden Pictures (t). **50 Alamy Stock Photo:** Stephen Dalton / Minden Pictures (tl). **naturepl.com:** Jane Burton (crb). **51 Dreamstime.com:** Ondej Prosick (bl). **Getty Images:** The Image Bank / Enrique Aguirre Aves (cr). **52 Dreamstime.com:** Johannes Gerhardus Swanepoel (t). **53 Alamy Stock Photo:** Andrew DuBois (b). **54-55 Alamy Stock Photo:** Tom Ingram (c). **56 Dreamstime. com:** Paul Reeves (b). **57 Alamy Stock Photo:** Arya Satya (t). **58 Dreamstime.com:** Lucaar (tl). **59 Dreamstime.com:** David Head (tl); David Des Rochers (cr); Tupungato (bl). **60-61 Alamy Stock Photo:** Szymon Bartosz (t). **61 Alamy Stock Photo:** Roy Waller (tc). **62 naturepl.com:** Alan Williams (cla). **62-63 naturepl.com:** Marie Read (t). **64 Alamy Stock Photo:** Avalon.red / Andy Rouse (tr); Nature Picture Library / Ben Cranke (bc). **65 naturepl.com:** Krijn Trimbos (br). **Julius Simonelli:** (tl). **66 Alamy Stock Photo:** BIOSPHOTO / Adam Fletcher (clb); Corbin17 (tr). **67 Alamy Stock Photo:** Danita Delimont / Adam Jones (br); Leonid Serebrennikov (cla). **68 Dreamstime.com:** Julian Schaldach (tr). **68-69 Alamy Stock Photo:** imageBROKER / Jrgen Mller. **70 naturepl.com:** Ripan Biswas (tr); Solvin Zankl (bl). **71 Getty Images / iStock:** RugliG (cra). **Science Photo Library:** Dante Fenolio (bl). **72 naturepl.com:** Ingo Arndt (c). **73 naturepl.com:** Barry Mansell (c). **74 Dreamstime.com:** Holger Karius (cr). **Getty Images:** Hearst Newspapers / San Francisco Chronicle / Jerry Telfer (cl). **75 Dreamstime.com:** Rouakcz (bl). **Getty Images:** Mark Wilson / The Boston Globe (tl). **76 Alamy Stock Photo:** Dave Keightley (c). **77 Alamy Stock Photo:** robertharding / John Alexander (c)

Cover images: Front: **Alamy Stock Photo:** Juniors Bildarchiv GmbH / Milse, T. tl, Nature Picture Library / Ingo Arndt tr; **naturepl.com:** Chien Lee bl, David Pattyn br; Back: **Alamy Stock Photo:** Corbin17 br, Robertharding / Christian Kober tr; **Dreamstime.com:** Anagram1 bl, Cathy Keifer tl

All other images © Dorling Kindersley

For further information see: www.dkimages.com

The authors would like to thank

Our inspiring - and inspired - creative team at DK. A huge drumroll for our editor, James Mitchem and assistant editor, Kieran Jones. Their warmth, wisdom, support, enthusiasm, patience, and vision are pure gold. Humble thanks too to the exceptional design team - Sonny Flynn, Charlotte Milner, Charlotte Jennings, and Bettina Myklebust Stovne. We felt listened to and guided at every step of our collaboration.

And to our illustrator, Asia Orlando - our thanks for bringing these pages alive. The energy of your work is infectious.

Lastly, Meriel sends thank-yous to Peter, Margaret, David, Finn, and Otto. And a "grrrrruff yip" to Betsy-Boo, her super talkative doggo! Boo reads minds, moods, and has at least five sounds and three gestures for "I'd rather like a treat, please". Genius.

DK would like to thank

Caroline Hunt for proofreading; Helen Peters for indexing; Laura Barwick for picture research; Sakshi Saluja and Nehal Vermafor image assistance.